Curly and the Big Berry

Tony Mitton
Illustrated by Andy Parker

Curly and Ladybird wanted the big berry.

“I can’t get the berry,”
said Curly.

“I can’t get the berry,”
said Ladybird.

"We can't get the berry,"
said Curly and Ladybird.
"Get on my shell," said Snail.

Curly and Ladybird pushed and pushed.
"We can't push the berry down," said Ladybird.

Curly and Ladybird pulled and pulled.
"We can't pull the berry down," said Curly.

"Help!" said Curly.
"Help!" said Ladybird.
Curly and Ladybird fell down.

Then they looked up at the big berry.
They didn't push.
They didn't pull.

The big berry fell down!